I0467665

Table of Contents

Introduction to Wealth

Those words would seem typical of someone who is already rich and well off, but that is a popular misconception. Whether large or small, any amount of money that you have should go through an exhaustive wealth management system - it is the lifeblood of any individual in the capitalist society we live in and we should keep an eye on it. The basics apply; if you can manage wealth manage money - and you would have learned the strategies and formulas that have brought the rich to where they are today.

Managing your money means putting parts of it into various investment opportunities. This can come in the form of the property market, currencies, precious metals, tradable commodities. A diverse portfolio is key to opening up multiple revenue streams that is both lucrative and can give you added security in case one or two of your investments fail.

Now here's the thing, you would think that to do such a thing, you would need vast amounts of money - but that's not true. Not in the slightest bit. The market for the modest trader and investor has opened up of late. The basics of wealth creation is that you should always find channels for small investments that will give you a good rate of return. For example, you may not be able to invest in newly mined gold or diamonds or even property for that matter, but you can put small amounts in companies that do, and earn a reasonable rate of return. And you have just eliminated a whole lot of risk from your portfolio.

It is these channels that anyone focused on creating wealth should know about. Opportunities are all over, both off line and on line for anyone to make money. That is the start we all need to take on bigger and even riskier investments that promise better returns. Your money should be making money for you at any point. It could be earning interest from a money market account, or it could be a return of investment on some small scale online trading you have done. Whatever you put in should yield you profit, no matter how many investments you have. If one isn't working out, shut it down and use the money to look into other areas.

That is the kind of money and wealth micro management we should all be looking into. And if you aren't sure of yourself and want to be guided along, help is always at hand. There are a few select wealth creation home programmes that give you the mindset of a millionaire. Success in this case can be taught and knowledge will drive ambition to heights never known before. Some of these programme authors have made millions due to effective wealth management - and they are willing to impart this knowledge to you. Do a bit of research and read a few testimonials, you should be able find one in no time.

The thing about the internet is that it is really big on reputation - word of mouth and referrals play a huge role in pointing people in the right direction.

We all want to think we are better off at each stage of our lives. But most people don't see this as wealth building. Considering that wealth is often equated with greed and selfishness, it's very easy to understand why.

Think about this. Wikipedia defines wealth as a quantity of things, possessions, valuables or resources owned by someone. That's a rather dry way to put it. But while the amount of wealth a person builds varies, it is still a natural outcome of living. This doesn't only apply to money or appreciable assets either. We all acquire things which add to our wealth.

As such, everyone should to take steps for securing their own future and accept that wealth is an important part of that future. Life is tenuous and things that seem permanent in our lives can come apart rather quickly. A better way to see wealth, then, is building a personal estate to help secure your own future.

The core of any estate is all of the things a person owns, so we all build a personal estate during the course of our lives, and we all end with some level of wealth. That's one reason it's so important to know that the personal acquisitions we make in our lives will ultimately either build security into our estate or add burden into it.

It only makes sense that everyone should take a serious and personal approach to wealth building. The reasons for building wealth may vary by individual but common to all of us are:

- Wealth gives us a dependable safety net in life
- Wealth provides options and choices when making important life decisions
- Wealth provides time to recover from unanticipated pitfalls
- Wealth increases our security in the retirement years

This leads to the first basic truth for building wealth, which is to immediately begin to live below your means! As you learn to personalize the importance of wealth and your own reasons for building an estate, you must consistently use this truth as the starting point on your road map to success.

This first principle of estate building must be followed now and forever. Regardless of your current income, regardless of future changes to your income, and regardless of changes to your family status and size, living on less than you earn is required. The path called "spending less than you earn" is your personal road to estate building and is your safety net in life.

Unfortunately, living within your means isn't accomplished without some pain. It requires tackling debt, a difficult task for many people. Controlling and eliminating debt, particularly consumer debt, is absolutely a necessary step toward living below your means. It must be done, pain or not, as nothing will tax your ability to save more than excessive debt.

Living on less than you earn has to be your cornerstone for building wealth and is the number one ingredient for ongoing wealth building. It allows you to grow a personal fund of dedicated money, which will be money set aside to be used as your primary tool for acquiring long-term assets.

There are many ways to invest dedicated money, including equities, fixed income investments, hard assets and others. All involve subsequent important principles to be learned only after the first principle is in place: spend less than you earn.

Living on less than you earn has to become a lifetime habit. Begin by saving something from every paycheck. Saving early in life is most important, but saving at any stage of life is important too.

The quickest means to spending less than you earn is to create a budget. Start with a simple budget. Basic budgeting tips and guides are abundantly found online and all help control personal spending. A popular personal finance site is Mint: Money Manager, Bill Pay, Credit Score, Budgeting... and it will help you with budgeting and eliminating debt.

Beyond just building your personal wealth, developing skills to guide your financial life is a true confidence builder and it bolsters your self-esteem. It becomes a feel good habit to have. The personal control and confidence you experience will be necessary for making wise decisions you'll use to increase your personal wealth.

While the core reason for planning and growing your own estate should always be personal security, living on less than you earn must always remain your number one principle of wealth building. Be assured it's a lifelong habit used by everyone who has watched their own estate increase. You can be successful experiencing your own abilities for building personal security. Your own wealth building begins today by living below your means.

Wealth Pillars

Everything in life has foundation or in simplest term, a start. You can imagine a newly born baby from its infancy to adulthood. You will agree with me that, there are series of processes and systems in term of growth that goes along with a child development from its first day on this earth to its adulthood.

Similarly, wealth is no difference from such process or system of growth. However, there are 4 basic wealth pillars which have been hidden from many people and a lot of these people always ask question about wealth acquisition or creation at a point in time. However, only few numbers of people have really discovered this in recent times.

Basically, these 4 wealth pillars are in everybody and everyone has what it takes to discover his/her own wealth. These 4 wealth pillars are as follow:-

- Knowledge-Intelligence
- Natural gifts
- Systems
- Attitude

Knowledge-Intelligence:

Knowledge is one of the 4 wealth pillars which are very vital in the process of wealth growth. Knowledge is power and it is the basis for any wealth creation. However, intelligence is the core substance that is very important to knowledge. Although, intelligence is independent of knowledge, but knowledge is dependent of intelligence. There are 3 basic forms of intelligence and they are;

- Natural
- Academic
- Artificial

Natural Intelligence:

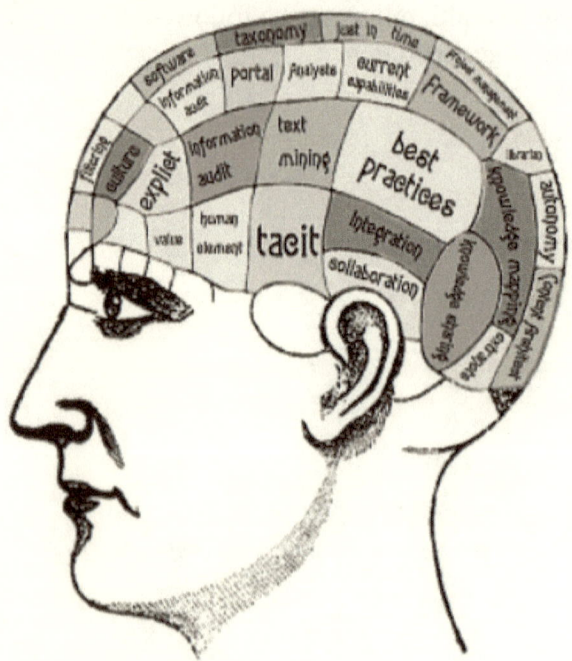

This is the natural endowment in everybody and it is a core drive to wealth growth. It may also be referred to as talents, potentials or gifts as the case may be. Most wealth creators always use their natural intelligence to grow their own wealth.

Academic Intelligence:

This form of intelligence is basically acquired through the school systems. From personal research, it is discovered that, this form of intelligence is dynamic in nature and changes over time. However, there are certain limits of this form of intelligence compares to natural intelligence. It is limited by human errors. 90% of the world wealth is being controlled by 10% of people around the world. As far as wealth is concerned, more emphasis should be placed on natural than academic intelligence. However, both natural and academic intelligence are essential for overall growth of human development.

Artificial Intelligence:

Artificial intelligence has been into existence, since the invention of different types of computers. The

advent of series of development in computer technologies has paved way to artificial intelligence (AI). It is this development that gives birth to Information, Computer and Technology (ICT). Thus, enhances the overall development in other areas such as, social, economy, and politics of any given nation that embraces such latest discovery. The use of internet also creates information age. We are in the information age, where the person that has the best information acquires great wealth.

Natural gifts:
As earlier mentioned, natural gifts has been responsible for great wealth around the world. Natural gifts also refer to potentials or talents as the case may be. And it is a drive to both wealth acquisition and growth.

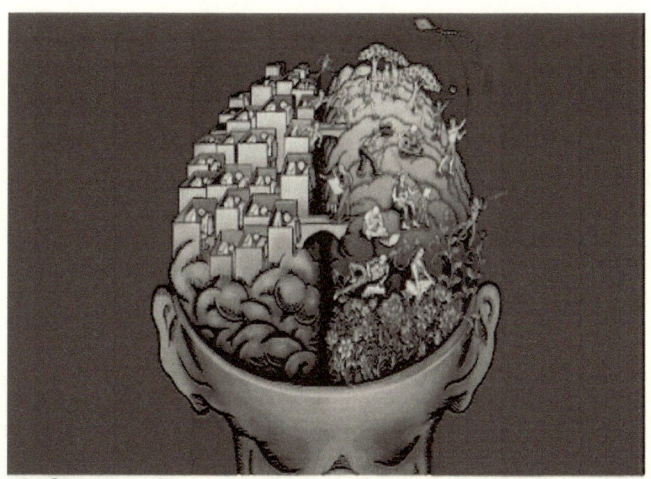

Unfortunately, many people have not discovered their talents and as a result, they are often operating below their real ability. However, when great potentials are being discovered earlier in life then, great wealth is often created with little or no effort.

There are 3 ways to discover your talents or potentials and they are;

- Passion
- Proactive
- Learning/Study

Passion:

When you find yourself doing a particular thing on a repeat basis and you derive joy, satisfaction and drive to do more, then it is likely that your gift has been discovered. Also, one thing about this passion is that, it will flow out naturally from you, even, if you are not being paid for such task.

Proactive:
In order to discover your gift, you need to be dynamic or active in what you strongly believe in and have passion for. This is because, at times, this so called gift needs to be stirring up.

Learning/Study:

You can critically study the various ways of doing your passionate task(s) which is (are) very dear to you. You can also understudy yourself for as long as you desire. Once you have done that and you are fully satisfied about the outcome of your results, then you have discovered your talent(s).

Systems: The basic routine of any wealth growth is the effectiveness and efficiency of derivable system(s) which must stand the test of time. Systems being one of the wealth pillars cannot be over emphasized. Simple systems of creating wealth are required not only for wealth growth, but also for long term stability of such wealth. An effective and efficient system gives rise to wealth accumulation.

Attitude: It is often said that, attitude determines the altitude of a person in life. This is no difference as far as wealth is concerned. Attitude means one's character toward one's passion and people generally. It reflects the nature of oneself toward life itself. Most often than not, many people desire to be wealthy, but over the years have been battling with one form of character crisis or the other.

Frankly speaking, character crisis has been the bane behind diminishing wealth in individuals and destroy many great talents. There are some forms of character crisis and they are; distrust dishonesty, ignorance, instability, laziness procrastination and lying.

Wealth is Not Measured in Millions

Isn't it? What is it measured in then? My banking friends would strongly insist that it is money, of course, you measure wealth in. Wealthy individuals are high net worth individuals, who simply have lots of money...millions.

Could there be another way of measuring wealth ? If you have seen the movie "The Secret" or read the

book, you might have heard one more definition of wealth: "it is not wealth to have lots of money when being unhappy and it is not wealth either to be 'spiritual' and broke all the time - life is meant to be abundant in all areas". Sounds nice, doesn't it ? I definitely want to believe it. And funny enough, the law of attraction, which "The Secret" movie is based on, proclaims exactly that: you get what you think about and believe in with all your heart.

So is wealth measured in money or abundance in all areas of life ? The advertising of a financial service organization a friend showed me recently, really spoke to me when it said: "Wealth is not measured in millions, it is measured in a feeling called freedom." What I like about this definition is that it puts money in its place as a means to an end rather than an end in itself. So is it the feeling of freedom, that defines our wealth ? I think there is some truth in this.

When you have enough money to cover your basic necessities (what that is exactly is entirely different topic), you are free ! You are free to choose how you want to live, which experiences you want to have in your life, whether you want to follow what your environment expects of you (e.g. making more money and upgrading your house, your car, your branded clothes and your private banker) or whether you want to follow your heart (and maybe have money come in as a side product). Of course, every choice you make automatically means a choice against something else, so it requires courage to stand up for one's choice. But choice you have. Choice is freedom.

You may have sensed it by now, there is something intensely subjective here about the feeling of freedom. Some people have much much more money than covering "basic necessities" and still don't feel free. They feel slaves to their possessions and commitments. Others have very little and feel free. Who is wealthier ?

If some people manage to (and hence it is possible to !) really feel free with just covering the basic necessities and if feeling free means wealth, shouldn't we all work on reducing what we define are our "basic necessities" in order to get to wealth faster ? Studies show that the opposite is happening. When a television set or a car was not defined as being "basic necessity" decades ago, several TV's and cars are now seen as basic necessity my many. Yet, studies also show that despite increased numbers of luxuries available to households in the developed world, happiness has not increased. So is it time for a paradigm shift ? Wealthy with less rather than more .?

I would like to offer another different view on wealth and this is my absolute favourite. The wealth of a person is the sum of that person's experiences. I love this definition because in difference to money, experience is the only thing nobody can ever take away from you.

The more of them you have and the more diverse they are, the more you learn, develop and grow as a person and that truly must mean being wealthy. People worry a lot about money, the money they don't have but also the money they have: they worry about losing it, protecting it, insuring it, investing it safely. People worry about money being taken away from them again.

Money (beyond basics necessities) does not make you free, it builds you a golden cage of responsibilities and brings with it fears of losing it again. Experience can't be taken away. Once you've got it, you have it FOREVER ! It is forever yours. And the more you have, the richer you become. Accumulating experiences (rather than money) makes you free: free of worry (there is nothing to lose) and makes you rich as an individual. The saying "a wealth of experience" hasn't been invented for nothing.

Wealth Building Program

Building wealth is imperative for all the business owners. Businesses should be established in such a way that diversified incomes are created. However, generation of profits should be prioritized here. To attain this goal, an appropriate wealth building program should be created. A portion of net profits should constantly be invested in some or the other investment instruments which would help in the production of sources that can be made available for present as well as long-term needs. Let some light be thrown on various advantages of chalking out a wealth building program.

Advantages

The first and the foremost source of income of yours is your business. There are several sources being made available for assisting you in the successful creation and operation of business worth millions of dollars. Certain businessmen would get there, certain won't. Some would be going way ahead. The way by which you would be earning money would be base in wealth building program of yours. Secondly, you should obtain expertise in understanding and controlling the finances of your business. This would be a key factor in attaining a healthy cash flow.

The next thing to be incorporated is gaining knowledge and understanding regarding all tax-free, taxable, and tax-deferred alternative streams of income, and optimizing them completely. Creation of a wealth building program would help you in working effectively towards financial objectives of yours, viz; obtaining financial freedom.

The main objective behind development of wealth building program is less dependence on business income. An appropriate business plan would be giving you freedom on the monetary basis and also safeguard against death, illness, inflation, etc. In other words, you turn out to be completely secured with respect to long-term and short-term wants and needs.

Revenue streams

Remember to ensure of three exclusive revenue streams before starting with the business. They would certainly benefit you a lot. These streams include net profits obtained from your business, income out of personal investments that could be obtained from dividends, bonuses, and salaries from the business of yours, and future income through several tax-deferred investments such as annuities and pension plans. Income streams cannot be e□uated with building wealth. These can be termed as a subset of the huge wealth building program.

Investment streams

The wealth building program of yours should be inclusive of investment streams such as mutual funds, stock options, forex, penny stocks, high-valued stocks, real estate, bonds, and collectibles such as silver and gold coins. Investing in any one of the above-mentioned instruments would risk your money. Diversification is the best alternative to avoid this risk.

The wealth building program of yours should begin with knowing the needs of yours. Along with that, you need to know the way of fulfilling these needs. There are many programs provided by software companies in this regard. Certain programs happen to be free as well. In short, wealth building program of yours must be inclusive of goals- short-time, middle-time, and long-time. Your business should be such that working on the annual basis for achieving long-term goals can be easily possible. You should be able to project certain amount of income every year, just like the government bonds. If you happen to have deficiency or back-log in the income of yours, you should know how to cover it up by the end of that year. As such, keep going with the wealth building program!

Principle of Building wealth

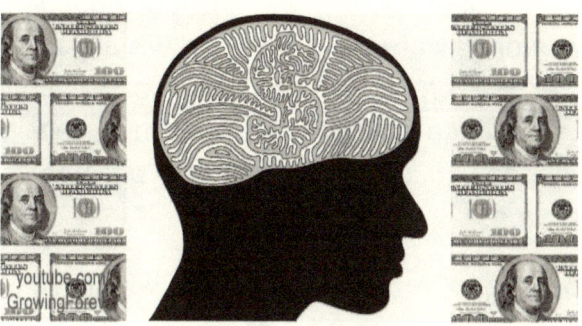

Let's quickly review the principles discussed in the first part of building wealth. We established that prosperity consciousness must first be developed mentally to acquire any real wealth.

A person that constantly worries about money most likely is living in scarcity consciousness regardless of the size of his or her bank account. We talked about some methods and daily exercises that can be employed to start developing a stronger level of prosperity consciousness.

The first exercise uses written affirmations, the second utilizes visualization, and finally we need to become more aware of how willing we are to give and receive prosperity on a daily basis. If we start using these methods, we'll begin to see gradual changes in our lives that will become larger over time.

As a follow-up to improving the way we think about wealth and prosperity, there are some effective money management techni□ues that will further support our prosperity consciousness. Certainly if we use the exercises discussed earlier in program, we'll start to view money differently, but those principles should be fortified by our actions as well. What we want to accomplish with our money is to generate a steady cash flow into our lives that will elevate our feelings of prosperity over time. The first step toward achieving this end is to simply pay ourselves first. Every time we get paid, we should save a portion of what we've earned. It's recommended that at least 10% of our pay be set aside for savings.

So if you already have a savings account, the big question is what is the purpose of this account? Is it for emergencies or a major purchase? Do you have more than one savings account? If we want to establish a consistent flow of prosperity, we must gradually build prosperity in our bank accounts while at the same time protecting ourselves against life's financial emergencies and obligations. It's very demoralizing to save a significant amount of money only to have to spend it on a costly emergency - the worst part is that often times, an event like this will knock us right off the prosperity track entirely. So we should strive to not only protect ourselves financially from these types of events, but more importantly, we must protect ourselves emotionally from these types of events.

The most effective way to handle our savings is to have more than one savings account with each having a different purpose. Although each of us will have different financial goals, it is recommended that everyone have a minimum of three different savings accounts with the following purposes:

1) **Emergency Funds** - This fund is set aside for those incidents that pop-up unexpectedly. Managing these events is critical to building wealth because they throw us off our budgets and demoralize us mentally. Unfortunately, emergencies are when many of us resort to credit cards, which makes this account even more critical. We MUST manage this aspect of our financial lives, otherwise life's little emergencies will continue to rob our wealth if we let them.

2) **Purchases** - This fund is used to save for major purchases such as a piece of furniture or a new car. In addition, we can also use these funds for buying Christmas or birthday gifts. These types of purchases are also occasions where many of us are inclined to use credit. It's not uncommon for Americans to be loaded with debt right after the Christmas holiday season. Just like the Emergency Fund account, the Purchases account is designed to keep us away from using credit.

3) **Wealth Building** - This last account is probably the most important if we manage it properly. There is only one rule for this account - the funds must never be spent. Never spent?!? Then what good is this account if it's never spent, you ask? Two reasons. The first reason is that we want this account to reach a level where we can eventually spend or even live off the interest it earns. Secondly, this account will be our biggest builder of prosperity consciousness. As this account grows in value, we'll become more and more comfortable with wealth coming into our lives. Have you ever noticed how money just seems to flow naturally to wealthy people? There's a reason for that - it's not coincidental, it's their attitude that attracts the wealth. So as this account grows and grows, so does our comfort with money and our willingness to receive abundance.

These accounts need not be savings accounts with your bank. In fact, most of them shouldn't be savings accounts. Obviously we want our funds earning as much interest as possible and we all know that savings accounts have probably the poorest yields of all.

One approach is to place our more liquid accounts such as Emergency Funds into savings accounts, perhaps keep our Purchases account in short term CD's since we can plan more easily for purchases, and then place our Wealth Building funds in a Mutual Fund. Again, the arrangement will be different for each of us - the important thing is to start setting them up.

The accounts mentioned here should be in addition to those that may be offered by your employer. Employer sponsored plans such as 401K's are a great way to supplement wealth building, but we still need to manage our wealth on a daily basis to establish a prosperous mindset. Keep in mind that the accounts mentioned here are a minimum. There are countless ways to use this approach. For instance, we may choose to have a Purchases account and then another account for Gifts. Or we may want to add another account called Vacations. Many money management pundits advise setting back 3-6 months worth of living expenses in the event of emergency unemployment. Perhaps when our emergency account gets big enough, we can place these "Emergency Unemployment" funds into a separate interest bearing account. Again, there are countless variations to using this approach.

Finally, one last note about maintaining the accounts. We mentioned earlier that setting aside 10% of your pay is a good minimum and a great level on which to start. Some of us may be able to save more, others may have to save less - the main thing is that we get started. In addition, a portion of any unexpected windfall should also go into savings. As far as how much of that savings should go into each account is up to each person. The simple approach is to split it e☐ually among all the accounts, but as situations arise, it may be practical to feed one account more than the others at times. This is fine as long as the rules for each account are strictly followed.

Remember - like it or not - our current finances are simply a reflection of our current level of prosperity consciousness. So if more wealth is desired, we must alter the way we're presently thinking about prosperity. If these Wealth Building principles and techniques are followed and we're persistent to this cause, it's guaranteed that real wealth will find its way to our lives over time.

7 Basic Rules to Building Wealth

1. Consistent discipline and attention to wealth

If you use a hit and miss approach to managing your wealth you will never build significant wealth. For most people building wealth is a gradual process over time which requires constant discipline and attention to detail. You must know how much return you get from investments as well as how much you are spending on everything to control those things. There is no substitute for this discipline and attentiveness.

Most wealthy people are keenly aware of where there money comes from and where it goes. If you want to build wealth you must do the same.

2. Never pay your bills first

One common distinction between poor people and rich people is that poor people try to pay all their bills and expenses first and then save what is left over. This does not work. You will inevitably spend all you earn and have nothing left over to save. The only way to insure that you will save is to do so before you pay the bills and to do so automatically and every month.

The amount you save every month is not as important as how consistently you do so.

3. Avoid consumer debt
There are two kinds of debt: investment debt which builds equity or wealth and consumer debt which builds nothing. If you incur debt to build a successful business or to buy a home you are building wealth over time. If you borrow to buy consumer items such as cars or furniture or clothing you build no wealth.

If you can limit your debt to investment debt you will go a long way toward building genuine wealth. This requires self denial. You must be willing to say no to purchases that you do not absolutely need to avoid this kind of debt.

4. Learn from successful people
Many people have built great fortunes having started out with nothing. Learn from them. Read books about them and by them and learn how they did it. What disciplines did they use? How much sacrifice were they willing to make now for long term wealth? Do they think in the short term or the long term? How hard did they work to build their wealth? What skills did they learn to increase their income?

Answers to questions like these will give you the tools to build wealth much as these people did.

5. Learn about taxes
For most wage earners their largest annual expense is taxes. Most people pay between 25% and 50% of their income in taxes. The more you know about how to legally reduce your tax burden the more money you will save and have available to invest.

Read books and consult with experts on how to minimize your tax burden. At first it may be a yearly visit to the tax preparer, but in time you may need a financial advisor and an accountant.

6. Avoid unnecessary expenditures
In Western society we are all urged constantly to buy the newest products and replace everything with the newest version. Before making any purchase think about it. Ask yourself if you really need it. Always give yourself a time period between your first impulse to buy and the final decision. You will find that most of the time as several weeks pass you either no longer want what you thought you wanted or you realize you can easily live without it.

Much of what makes life truly worth living has nothing to do with what you can buy. Focus on those things in life that are free but valuable, like your relationships. By continuously limiting your purchases of unnecessary things you will save thousands of dollars over time.

7. Build a Business
There is no substitute for the cash flow that a successful business can provide. Most wealthy people own one or more businesses. It is very difficult to become wealthy on an hourly wage. For some it is impossible. But a successful business can generate constant surplus income which will build wealth.

8 Ways to Build Wealth

I've always been fascinated with how to build wealth and why some people have lots of money and others don't. So when I started a financial education business and people told me money matters were boring, I really had to think about their perspective. I concluded they were right...I mean if I viewed money as it's taught - all columns of numbers and like an accountant, then I'd think it was boring too. But for me, it was never about that. I'm not a number cruncher (I hated accounting in business school).

I'm a visual and creative person. I experience relief letting my accountant save me from the drudge of dealing with the number crunching as much as you do!

In the investment industry that I was a part of for over 25 years, it involved talking in a "foreign language" that made it seem complex. At the time I didn't think about it that way, but now that I'm free of the industry and look back on it, it was so unnecessary to speak in jargon. Now I teach about growing wealth in a way that doesn't use jargon, is not biased, and is from the perspective of what works.

So here's what I believe are the best ways to build wealth now:

1. **Separate financial education from offering investments**. If the pharmaceutical industry was in charge of teaching about health, then the answer would always be to take a prescription. Ergo, if the investment industry is teaching personal finance, then the answers usually involve buying an investment. The truth is, building wealth involves 7 other steps besides investing.

2. **Follow the steps to build wealth step-by-step.** There are 8 steps to build wealth, I believe, and they answer the □uestion, "How do I become rich?" The 8 steps are: create a wealthy mindset, save a nest egg, find a mentor, invest in money engines, compound at a high rate, leverage wisely, protect your wealth, give and create your legacy. You may have heard them before, but each step has many parts (beyond the obvious) and most people aren't doing them. There's an ancient Chinese proverb: "To know and not yet do, is to not yet know." If you do all 8 steps, in my opinion, you will become wealthy. It's exactly the step-by-step system I followed to become a millionaire at age 38. It works.

3. **Your "portfolio" isn't just your retirement plan or your IRA, it's how you spend the money that flows through your fingers**. Even the most modestly paid wage earners will earn $1 million in their lifetime, but how much becomes permanent wealth? It's mainly dependent on buying the "right" assets early. Just ask someone who bought a house in 2007 if that was the right time to buy a house or if 2000 was the right time to buy tech stocks to build wealth. Long-term, buying the right assets while they are growing is paramount.

4. **You don't have to be frugal, live in squalor, or forgo designer brands to build wealth.** Yes, you can have it all if you understand "value" and "building equity". I buy my Jimmy Choos at the outlet, shop wholesale, and buy Quality cars a couple of years old, in immaculate condition, that can be in style and last for a decade or longer!

5. **You don't need to "buy and hold" stocks and bonds over your lifetime.** There have been many 20 year periods in history where major stock indexes went down in value. How can you build wealth in an asset that goes down in value for 20 years? My wealth has come from identifying where the money is moving, getting there first before everyone else figures it out, and getting out before it peaks. I do this by identifying the next bubble, confirming with cycle forecasting it's the right trend, and using my own system to identify when a bubble will peak. Are you aware of an investment that has grown about 16% a year for the last 9 years, with a positive return every year (even 2008)? Most people don't own it in their portfolio yet, but a few years from now when it's peaking I'll bet will be clamoring for it.

6. **Buy assets that will go up in value**. Some of my clients have incomes of $250,000+, but they have no appreciating assets. They're mired in debt from buying multiple residences, boats, and new cars - all depreciating assets. You cannot build wealth if you don't have appreciating assets.

7. **Forget popped bubbles and buy into the next bubbles early**. Bubbles that have popped don't re-inflate anytime soon. For example, Nasdaq tech stocks are still 50% below where they were 10 years ago. Cycles show real estate won't be re-inflating to old prices for a long time. Forget popped bubbles like real estate, move on to the next bubbles early to grow your wealth!

8. **In the New Economy,** you have to think differently and invest for the future, instead of looking in the rear view mirror. That's how billionaires like John Paulson, who made $4 billion in one year by investing in the anticipated future trend of a crashing subprime mortgage market, invest. Start using forward vision to build your wealth.

In my opinion, the largest transfer of wealth in history is about to occur in the next few years. Now is the time to learn the new ways to build wealth and own the next appreciating assets.

The Master Key to Building Wealth in Business and Your Personal Life

The master key to attracting wealth and success in business and your personal life lies in your ability to master two forgotten skills that's free to everyone -relaxation and focus. Yet most people are under the impression that they must constantly remain busy or always take some sort of action to create wealth.

True, some sort of action on your part is necessary, but that is a small part. The most difficult and largest portion of your time should be spent:

1) Deciding what it is you want, not what you don't want.

2) Learning how to relax your mind and body.

3) Focusing on your objective until you attract it to you.

When you learn to master these three steps, you are deliberately using the Law of Attraction to create what you want to experience, with very little effort.

There are many great people who have lots of energy, drive, and ambition, but they lack direction! This lack of direction has created confusion in their lives. Consequently, their lives look and feel like a mental junk shop.

As a human being, you are a magnetic field of mental influence. Your thoughts attract certain circumstances and events into your life based on what you habitually think about. This is not an opinion -- this is a proven fact.

Through the Law of Attraction, you automatically magnetize or attract to you the things you constantly dwell upon. Your mind, which functions like a computer, re☐uires efficient and positive programs fed into it on a regular basis.

To successfully build wealth into your business or personal life re☐uires that you feed your mind wealth-building concepts on a regular basis. The most effective way to accomplish this is to learn how to relax the body and mind on a daily basis.

When you master this skill, you will be on your way to building wealth and anything else you want to experience in your life.

The Importance of a Wealth Building System

Today, the world is not as stable as most people would like it to be and is the reason the wealth building system was created. This is because economies are on the downturn, and most people are not as secure as they would like to be in their jobs. In addition, this applies to those in the private sector as well as those in the central government.

That is why they are turning to other methods of earning more income. This is so that they can be stable and provide security for their families. In fact, it is the main motivation behind the fact they look for new sources of income; hence the popularity of the wealth building system.

How the wealth building system works

One of the ways in which people have realized that they can earn more cash is by using this one of a kind system. It is contrived such that it can make any person start a home business successfully and in an extremely easy manner. Therefore, it re□uires little expertise to start it off. This is unlike most systems available today.

The wealth building system is also designed in such a way that mentor ship can be provided to individuals who feel that they cannot go it alone. These mentors are well trained and provide guidance on every step of the way once a person decides that they will join the wealth building system. The mentors who are given to every new person who joins the system do not only offer guidance on how the system works. Rather, they also give advice on pertinent issues in life so that one may live to the fullest.

The wealth building system for newbies

Just like many other business systems or units, there are steps that ought to be followed for them to work. Moreover, with aid from wealth masters international experts, a person can be able to achieve anything that they want. All one needs is to follow the instructions given, and they are guaranteed to succeed.

As a matter of fact, the wealth building system has even been designed for newbie's who have no idea on what marketing or advertising entails. Therefore, anyone who wants to make use of the system can do so. In addition, if they keep at it for long enough they are guaranteed to be experts themselves after some time. That is how well the system works and is also the reason the success rate is high too.

The reason the wealth building system is suited for anyone

Therefore, anyone who feels that they are not secure in their jobs may turn to this program so that they can change their lives for the better. Additionally, since the wealth building system ensures that one can grow their income stream as long as they work on it, the program offers continuous education too.

The education is provided so that a person can learn the newest methods that they can use in the system. As such, a person is assured that the program will always work since they too are changing with the times. Thus, the wealth building system is recommended for people who need to live life more fully, with no stress. Living a life of prosperity and attracting health, wealth and wisdom into our lives requires us to collectively become a part of the SOLUTION! It starts with us. Wealth Masters International is a solution to the current economic crisis. We are changing lives each and every day.

Learn the Power of Accumulation to Build Wealth

Financial success comes from the power of accumulation. This power has to do with how adding a little on a constant basis can build into a fortune over time. It requires the vision to see where small efforts every day can lead to great accomplishments over time. Learn this and apply it and you will realize tremendous accumulation of wealth.

Nature is Our Teacher

Nature teaches us the value of gradual accumulation. While some natural processes such as volcanic eruptions and earth ▢uakes can massively change the landscape in a short time most of the change that occurs in nature occurs through gradual accumulation.

Mighty glaciers hundreds of miles across are built one tiny snow flake at a time. Thousands of miles of beaches are made up of billions and billions of grains of sand, each one eroded from stone by wind and water, one at a time. The immense Grand Canyon was eroded by wind and water one millimeter at a time over millions of years. In fact most of the face of the earth was carved and formed from the gradual forces of tiny rain drops and snowflakes. Never underestimate the power of the constant force of tiny steps repeated over and over.

Accumulate Value Not Stuff

When we speak here of accumulation we are not talking about stuff. No one becomes wealthy buying lots of stuff. Millions have s◻uandered thousands of dollars on consumer items. They hold no value and they bring no return. When we speak here of accumulation we speak of accumulation of wealth through the discipline to save on a constant basis and to wisely invest what has been saved.

Value Investment Rather Than Status

Part of the pressure that causes many to spend their hard earned money on stuff is that they think it buys them status. People want to drive expensive cars and houses, wear lots of expensive clothing and own lots of recreational toys because it brings them status. It is however a hollow status. It does not endure. The stuff that people spend their money on holds little value in most cases and earns no return.

If you invest your money in value rather than in status you will see great returns over time. Like tiny snowflakes those dimes and ◻uarters you save and invest will over time create massive fortunes.

One Small Step After Another Will Travel a Thousand Miles

The great Chinese philosopher Lao Tzu is often credited with the axiom A Journey of a Thousand Miles Begins With a Single Step. He may as well have said that a journey of a thousand miles is made up of many single steps. People have walked around the world but have done so one step at a time.

You can build wealth in the same manner, one dollar at a time. People are by nature inpatient. They want to see immediate results. They want immediate gratification. People do not want to wait decades to see the gradual accumulation of their investments turn into a fortune. They want it now.

For most of us however it will not happen now. It will only happen over time. I once suggested to someone that if they invested carefully and lived more frugally they could create significant wealth in as little as ten years. The response was total surprise and frustration. Who wants to wait ten years was their response. I then suggested to them that the ten years will pass one way or the other.

Ten years from now you can be just as poor as you are today if you do nothing differently. However, if you apply the discipline to save and invest on a regular basis over those ten years when they have passed you will have a tidy sum.

Many people look back over their lives and wonder where the time and the money went. They lacked the vision to use discipline today to build the fortune of tomorrow.

Learn from nature and from those who have applied the power of accumulation. Begin today to save and to invest. Day by day, dollar by dollar, it will grow. It may take a decade, it may take more than one decade, however long it takes, the time will pass either way, in the end you will either have a fortune or you will have nothing. The vision you have today and the discipline you apply over the time that passes will make the difference.

Secrets of Getting Rich

There are three fundamental secrets to getting rich. If you do not know these secrets or do not put them into practice, you will not get rich. Period.

There are several secrets to getting rich, but these three are absolutely fundamental. If you do not employ them, you will not get rich.

In interviews with those who have gotten rich, most of these people did not realize they used these secrets. But they did. Each and every person who has achieved great wealth has used these secrets even if they did not know they were doing so.

They may have felt that it was just a natural way of doing business or that it was something they had to do or that it was just "natural" or however else they may have labeled it. But by whatever label, everyone who has achieved riches has employed these three secrets. If you want to get rich, you will use these secrets also.

Using these three secrets is so important because their use will almost guarantee that you will achieve the riches you seek. Conversely, the opposite is also true; not using these secrets will almost guarantee that you do not attain the riches you desire.

The first secret is sharing. Ok, I know this may seem adolescent in nature, but every great business or wealthy individual employs this secret. Sharing means the distribution of a product or service to the greatest number of people possible. It does not mean you give it away. In fact, the term "sharing" as we are using it here implies that you are charging a high - but fair - premium for your product or service. You charge a premium for two reasons. One is that perception is everything in the marketplace.

The higher the value you place on your product or service the higher the value of that product or service will be perceived by those who seek it. The second reason you charge a premium is because you are delivering a high ☐uality product or service and the value you have assigned to it is worth the premium you are charging.

We will not consider how to identify or develop a product or service, nor will we consider the marketing aspect of sharing, each of these subjects would re☐uire at least a separate article or even a book to consider fully. Just remember that the first secret of how to get rich is sharing which means finding or developing a high ☐uality product or service that people want and delivering that to as many people as possible.

The second secret is leverage. If you try to get rich by yourself, it won't happen unless you win a lotto or big win in Vegas or receive an inheritance. The reason you won't get rich by yourself is that there are simply not enough hours in the day to do everything that is re☐uired to get rich by yourself. In addition, you do not have all the skills, knowledge, education, experience or resources necessary to get rich.

No one does. No one ever has. Where these things are lacking, you hire, team up, joint venture or partner with those who have the time, skills, experience and resources you do not.

Focus on your strengths and build on them. Leverage out your weaknesses (including financial re☐uirements). Let others focus on their strengths while you focus and develop your own. Only by focusing on your strengths can you get rich. The more you can use your strengths and develop them while leveraging out your weaknesses the faster and the greater the wealth that will flow to you.

Secret number three is clearing. Clearing means two things. Do either one and you will get rich. Do both and your riches will be multiplied.

The first part of clearing means to know what you want and focus on that to the exclusion of all else. You must have a vision of what your goal will look like and you must concentrate all effort on that eliminating all distractions and impediments that may hinder, prevent or delay your goal of getting rich.

Clearing also means to clear yourself of the negative thought patterns, memories and belief states that are directing your thoughts and actions and controlling your destiny. One of the reasons - and perhaps the only reason - you are not already rich is because your belief states, thoughts and memories have prevented you from attaining the riches you desire.

How to Create Wealth Using Harmony

To be able to create wealth, one first needs to understand the true meaning of the word wealth. The word wealth in its original form means to have all round well being in your life. There are seven different areas of your life in which you will need to experience well being and growth in order to be able to create wealth. Your ability to do this effectively will lead to your having a life filled with harmony and abundance.

The seven areas of your life which I am referring to make up what is known as the wheel of life and your ability to keep these areas growing in harmony with one another is the secret to creating wealth. The seven areas are:

1. Vocational
2. Financial
3. Family
4. Social
5. Mental
6. Physical
7. Spiritual

It will be your ability to grow and improve all seven of these areas of the wheel of life which will determine the rate at which you will be able to create wealth in your life. By striving to make small but constant improvements to each of these areas of your life on a daily basis, you will soon realize that by keeping them in harmony and constantly growing you will be creating wealth on a daily basis in your life.

The reason these areas of your life need to be in harmony is simple, if you are not growing them in harmony with one another, there will be an imbalance in your life. The moment this occurs the area which is shrinking will cause the others to shrink as well, but the opposite is also true. If all areas are growing, they will benefit the others to do the same.

Getting your wheel of life balanced is instrumental in your ability to create wealth and make it sustainable. So long as you are making small but constant changes in order to improve your overall wealth, the easier it becomes for you to become wealthy.

How To Attract Wealth in 3 Simple Steps

Almost everybody probably wants to know how to attract wealth into their lives. It doesn't really matter where you are right now or what situation you may face in the future, everybody has the exact same opportunity in front of them to learn the exact techniques involved to attract all the wealth they will ever need.

So read on as I reveal to you the simple 3 step process that I and countless other successful business people use to attract massive wealth.

Step 1. Mindset is Everything.

If you truly would like to learn how to attract wealth into your life, then you need to focus on your mindset first. What do I mean by this. Well, in the financial world there are only 2 mindsets you can adopt, these are a wealthy mindset or a poverty mindset. So what's the difference between them?

Let's talk about a wealthy mindset first: Rich people generally have a wealthy mindset. You only need to listen to the conversations that rich people have to understand this. They talk about abundance, prosperity, and making more money. They see opportunity not obstacles. They always find ways to make more money.

Now listen to a poor persons conversation: They talk about never having enough, how the government doesn't do enough to help, how it is never their fault. They always see obstacles and reasons why they can't make any money.

You see the difference right away. What you think about comes about. If you think and talk about "lack" then you will receive more "lack". However, if you think and talk about "abundance" then you will attract the wealth of abundant opportunities - that exist all around you - into your life.

Step 2. Gratitude is The Key.

Start every day by being grateful for what you have. Start your day with this affirmation: " I am so happy and grateful now for all that I have in my Life Right Now!"

Be grateful everyday for the food that you eat, the home you live in and even the air that you breathe.

Repeat this next affirmation by a mentor of mine, Bob Proctor, at least 6 times a day (and get as many other people to say it on a daily basis as well, as you can) " I am so happy and grateful now that money comes to me in increasing quantities, from multiple sources, on a continuous basis"

Finally, end every day with this affirmation " I am so happy and grateful now that I am succeeding in everything I do "

Then immediately before you go to sleep, write down 5 things that you are grateful for having in your life. Count blessings not sheep.

Gratefulness works in conjunction with generosity, so having this abundance mindset will probably mean that you will find yourself being more generous to people around you. Your positive nature will also attract to you more like minded people as well, which of course will result in more conversations about wealth, which will attract more wealth into your life, and what a wonderful cycle of wealth attraction that is!

Step 3. Your Wealth Attraction Plan

To some people wealth is only about money. I will tell you that those people may well become wealthy from a monetary point of view, but spiritually they are probably not. You know the type, the egotistical businessman who is always boasting about his latest "deal" or the self-satisfied salesperson glorifying their latest commission pay check.

To the truly Wealthy person, it isn't just about the money. Wealth can come in the form of family, friendships and happiness etc, if your plan to become wealthy does not include a spiritual aspect it will not be long lasting. So create your wealth attraction plan by following these next few steps:

a). Write down exactly what you want. (and make it BIG and SCARY)
b). Read it every day.
c). Be grateful for what you have.
d). Look for opportunities to mix with rich people, who share your ideals.
e). Never, Ever, Ever give up on your dreams.

Finally, don't get comfortable, never settle for second best, and remember for you to have more you have to "be" more. So get out of your comfort zone, release yourself from the "pity party" open yourself up to the endless possibilities that exist and attract wealth into your life now!

How To Turn Into the Essence of Wealth

What does true wealth feel like? As you focus on attracting wealth into your life, you will find it helpful to spend time each day attuning your awareness to the very essence of wealth.

The essence of wealth would be the way it feels when you think about it. What does it feel like to have more than enough money? What does it feel like to have a bank account filled to the brim? What does it feel like to live in your dream home? What does true financial freedom feel like?

When you can tune into these feelings on a regular basis, you will be attuning your own vibrational fre□uency to wealth, and begin attracting more of it into your life.

But what if you have trouble tuning into wealth? What if you've never been wealthy and don't know what it feels like?

Try the following exercise:

Decide on a sum of money that would make you feel wealthy if you had it right now. Perhaps a million dollars, or maybe even a smaller sum like $5,000 would make you feel wealthy.

Focus on this sum of money for a few moments and imagine that it was sitting in your bank account right now. How would that change the way you feel about your life? Would you feel more relaxed because you could easily cover all of your monthly expenses? Would you feel more secure because you could handle any emergencies that came up in the near future?

Focus on these feelings of security, peacefulness, well-being, and freedom. Immerse yourself in these feelings and enjoy them! It doesn't matter if you don't really have the money in the bank, because you will be emitting a vibrational frequency to the universe that says "I feel wealthy - I love feeling wealthy - please send me more situations that make me feel this good." And the universe will.

However, be sure to tune into wealth in this way as often as possible; once a day at a minimum but you can also do this exercise dozens of times each day and speed up the arrival of your wealth.

The wealthier you can feel on a regular basis, the more wealth you will attract!

Ways to Discover the Key to Attracting Wealth

A lot of debate takes place when it comes to matters related to money. For some of us Money Matters!! In some way or the other it relates to our needs, personal values, self-esteem, security, joy, happiness, fulfillment etc. We spend a lot of our time working towards accumulating money in order to fulfill our dreams and desires. All said and done, for most people money is something they do not seem to have enough at any point of time. They continue to seek more and more!

Let us consider this. Do you have to struggle everyday to receive money on a regular basis, or does it flow to you effortlessly so as to meet your monthly expenses or any emergency needs?

Looking at your life's experience will reveal your mindset about money and wealth. Are you able to attract money into your life? This is the Law of Attraction.

The Law of Attraction is activated by your mind-set. What you think and the way you think, believe, and feel on a regular basis is what activates your mind-set. Basically, it is your thoughts that trigger your emotions, which in turn emits a kind of wavelength or fre☐uency of energy into the universe. The universe in turn, returns events and experiences into your life, that correspond with your emotional fre☐uency.

Your thoughts play a major role in attracting anything positive and negative. When you think and feel positively on a regular basis, everything in your life seems to flow more easily, including money. However, when your thoughts are negative in nature on a regular basis, you experience problems, setbacks and financial distress.

Your beliefs also play a major role. The more you keep believing that you have to work hard to have lot of money, you'll create exactly that situation in your life.

If you believe that you do not deserve more than a certain amount of money, you will be creating a blockage of more money coming to you.

Whatever therefore are your thoughts and beliefs, your subconscious mind will create those events or moments over and over until you learn to change your thought process. You will need to clear some mind clusters or reorganize certain things in your life or do things differently in order to attract wealth.

Understanding the above principles and implementing it regularly will open the doors that welcome more money and happiness into your life.

Wealth Management

The term **"wealth management"** is really such a loaded one these days. When speaking of wealth, most people think about money.

True success isn't just about financial gain. Everyone has fixed ideas about wealth, and everyone wants to know how to protect their wealth. Looking at the big picture, however, the key to wealth management has little to do with just investing funds properly.

Perhaps the real problem that so many people have with wealth management is the fact that they do not understand what real wealth is. They do not understand where the source of their wealth lies, and they spend their entire lives looking for that source in places where it does not exist. The first step in wealth management is to understand that the true source of wealth actually lies within you!

If you're like most people, you have probably spent an adequate amount of time seeking wealth in your job, your relationships, or something else that you felt was important. Of course, these things certainly are important, but they do not provide the lasting source of wealth.

They will make you happy for a while, but seeking happiness outside of yourself will only rob you of true happiness and true wealth. It's pretty hard to practice wealth management if you haven't uncovered The Source of wealth in you.

Just think of your inner source of wealth as your own, personal buried treasure. You may need to dig deep to discover it. However, God has given you a uni□ue gift, and it is up to you to uncover it and to reveal it as the source of wealth, both for yourself and to the world in live in. After all, God is within, and you're the true source of wealth. The energy within you is what feeds your inner source of wealth, gives it life, and sustains it. Only when you reconnect with God will you reconnect to The Source of wealth in you.

The Path of Wealth Management

As you begin to tap into your inner source of wealth, you will notice a major change-- in yourself, in the way you treat others, in the way they treat you, and the type of people that begin to show up in your life. Wealth management will not be effective until the connection to the Source within is fully realized.

So, how can you realize that connection with God and your inner source of wealth? You must take control of your life, your mind, your thoughts, addictions, ego and your destiny.

Remember, God is energy, and you are made of energy, too. God gave you the beginning, but the continuation is up to you. Learning and daily application of the simple laws of the Universe is a must if you want to live a rich and meaningful life.

The problem is that many people allow someone or something else to control their destiny. They do anything they can to avoid personal growth through addictions or material happiness, and they allow those things to control them. Instead of being strong and living a life based on a strong foundation, values, and principles, they are flopping about in the wind like a weed out on an open field.

The wind blows them around, and they are unable to find happiness or true wealth because they can't control their own lives.

Taking Life off Cruise Control

You're like a car with cruise control. You can choose to set the speed that you want and then let go of the wheel. If you do that, you may cruise along at breakneck speed for a few feet, but you won't go far before you'll end up going off the road. You also have the opportunity to grab that steering wheel and correct your course, placing control right in the palm of your hand.

Taking control of your life is simply a matter of choice and it comes through co-creating your life. Once you make that conscious choice to take control of your life, then it's only a matter of time before you rediscover and reconnect to happiness and wealth. Wealth management is appreciating all that you've been blessed with. Decide whether you want to literally create what you need in your life or if you just want to cruise along.

The Beginnings of Wealth Management

Once you have wrenched control away from whatever else you were allowing to control your life, then you will begin to exercise true wealth management. You'll automatically start to act like and be your true self. In the process, you'll learn how to manage your wealth of personal gifts properly. The rest will naturally fall into its place.

You are an amazing creation, and the key to wealth management lies inside of you.

Uncover the treasures that hold your wealth. Make sure that you are managing the real source of wealth and not some bogus temporary source that lies outside of you and is based solely on material things. Don't be fooled exclusively by the material that some people think holds wealth. Instead, remember where your true source of wealth is.

You already know everything that you need to know about wealth management. Just spend some time rediscovering that knowledge. Then, get out and apply it by taking action, because knowledge without application is useless.

People have different reasons for contacting advisors. They include:

- **Planning for education-**This is even more important as tuitions rise and the job market becomes more selective, making a college degree even more important. Here, an advisor may recommend plans such as state-by-state 529 plans, or other investments depending upon your time horizon.

If you are expecting to be hit with college expenses for a child and have less than 10 years to invest-with nothing saved-talking to a wealth management advisor now is a good idea!

- Minimize taxes-This is especially true for those reaching higher brackets as their income increases. Here, an advisor might suggest a variety of tax-deferred investments that will give you income upon retirement (when you might be in a lower bracket).

- Portfolio performance-Some judge this by getting the highest returns, while others view it as more important to protect a portfolio from loss. Don't believe anyone who can guarantee performance-no one can. Instead, ask about investing philosophy and examples of how they've managed client portfolios in good and bad times, to gauge how your own portfolio might be managed

- Help define goals-This is especially helpful for couples who may have different attitudes about money-working with a professional (who is objective and outside the relationship) can be ☐uite helpful in creating a long-term plan that both investors can believe in.

Regardless of your reasons, many investors find that working with an advisor has positive long-term effects on their finances, investments, and long-term wealth management strategies.

Wealth Management For Managing Your Finance

In the field of wealth management, wealth refers to anything you possess which has a monetary value. Besides money, it could include property, shares and even a rare coin collection. It includes managing investments and financial planning, estate planning, financial banking, etc.

Today's times brings with it a pressure to increase income in order to maintain your lifestyle. Since it's impossible to outrun the rate of inflation, wealth management is essential in order to maintain your fundamental amount. Another reason that wealth management may be necessary is that high net worth individuals may prefer to keep their attention on their busy schedule. In this way wealth management is different from asset management because asset management primarily involves growing assets like money, stock, shares, bonds, etc to create a diverse portfolio in which it may increase in value. Wealth management is a larger umbrella that includes this as well as the maintenance of the principle amount and saving on tax through financial investment services. It re□uires an understanding of how markets operate and one has to stay abreast of financial news in order to have wealth be optimized.

There are several ways to go about managing wealth. Like life insurance policies that allow you to plan for a disaster or death, save on tax and increase the monetary value on the principle amount.

They work as both protection and investment. There are other insurance policies that function as both protection and investment, and include term plans, children's plans, pension plans, etc. Another way is tax planning. This includes understanding the tax deductions available on anything from income to interest received on a bank account to returns on investments. Equities, derivatives, real estate funds, commodity trading, estate planning and even art investments are all kosher in wealth management.

When you approach an entity to manage your wealth, they typically walk you through a process. At first, your assets and liabilities are analyzed along with your income and expenditure, and investments. Next, you are counselled on understanding your goals and aspirations. Both for the short-term as well as long-term. Then you may be counselled to understand what kind of commitment it takes to surrender your assets to products like various investments. In this way you can understand how best you feel comfortable to take on commitments for your assets that are designed to help you meet your goals.

Once you are advised on investment vehicles and any other action, it is up to you to decide whether you would like your wealth manager to act without your constant approval.

Wealth Masters International Growth Demands Attention

Wealth Masters International has been experiencing record growth numbers in 2009. With most companies feeling the s□ueeze, how is Wealth Masters doing it? We are going to talk about the real reasons for company growth in a second. First, let's do a quick Wealth Masters International review. Simply put, WMI is a financial education company offering first class training in the areas of wealth creation, money management and financial education.

Now, whether it's WMI or another company, this sort of "education" is in high demand (as it should be). As a society, we have to take the time to learn about money, finance and investing and quite frankly this is a topic that has been ignored by most. As a result, many have decided to "trust" other people with our money and we all know what happened as a result of that decision in late 2008. People are starting to face the facts about financial education, the demand for education and training is steady on the rise. This is one of the first reasons for Wealth Masters growth.

The co-founders, Kip Herriage and Karl Bessey have come from diverse backgrounds. Kip spent decades on Wall Street and is proud to say he retired from that life years ago.

Karl's reputation as an entrepreneur and a marketer has brought a dimension to WMI shaping their product line.

WMI offers some of the most marketable financial education products on the market today. Together Kip and Karl have grown their Texas based direct sales company to an international phenomenon. The company experienced a spike in sales because of a decision made back in 2006 that changed WMI forever.

Wealth Masters International continues to grow month over month as I write this, and will continue to provide top-tier financial education through its 3 flagship products, the M1, M2 and M3. WMI is in the industry of Top-Tier direct sales providing their consultant with high commission sales opportunities. Top Tier direct sales has become a highly sought after industry with a "hefty" pay out, but it still has the benefits of a small home based business. Many consider top tier direct sales to be the best of both worlds.

What Is the Power in Material Wealth in Good or Difficult Economic Times?

What is it about material wealth that attracts and captivates you? Exclude how it provides for your basic needs and ask yourself: What is the attraction I feel toward material wealth?

At the surface are obvious answers, some of which may or may not apply to you. Answers include: obtaining a status symbol, keeping up with your friends or neighbors, or just simply collecting wealth. However, when you look deeper at the root of these answers, you will find that the reason material wealth attracts you is because material objects bring instantaneous sensual pleasures to you. You can immediately see, touch, hear, taste, and smell when you ac□uire certain material possessions. However, pleasure arising out of material possessions is fleeting-it soon disappears. You can't help it; that is the nature of material wealth. To experience again a similar pleasurable experience, you move on to ac□uire your next material possession.

No shortage of material possessions are in the world. New and more attractive material offerings are introduced into the market every day. It is easy to choose your next possession. When full of desires, your mind is completely engaged with the material world to fulfill those desires. If you accomplish your desire by acquiring the material object, you derive instant pleasure from it.

But if you fail, you experience instant pain, anger, and failure. Pleasure and pain are two sides of the same coin. Either way, the nature of material wealth is to give you instant gratification or instant discontent. Instant gratification is what captivates you and drives you to acquire one more material possession, despite the risk of failing and experiencing pain or discontent. In fact, this balancing act is what makes life's journey more fun and interesting.

After you acquire material wealth, initial attraction over time turns into an attachment. Mind you, the attachment in itself has absolutely no pleasure in it. The pleasure came during the short period after the acquisition. After that short period, emotions of feverish excitement and pleasure settle down, and slowly, they give way to possessiveness. You start to develop a certain degree of attachment to your material possessions.

The degree of that attachment depends upon the value you and the market place on each of your possessions. As the market value goes up or down, so goes the state of your mind. You want to protect what you already have.

Because of sheer attachment, the risk of losing any possession creates anxiety and fear in your mind. In the beginning, material wealth captivated you. Now it holds you captive. That is the power material wealth holds over you. But you have the ability to take your power back. You must discover and develop this ability in you, especially in difficult economic times.

In this challenging economic climate, your family may experience reduced income, shrinking savings and, perhaps, a significant lifestyle change. As the economy and your finances struggle, Rakesh Sethi shares secrets of enjoying the wealth you have and asks readers to remember that there's more to life than material wealth. Simultaneously down-to-earth and inspiring, "Cruising Through Turbulence" book reminds you that your wellbeing is not connected with material wealth. The author encourages you to tap into your inner strength to sustain you and your family through any crisis, including difficult economic times

Wealth Attraction Techniques You Can Start Right Now

Wealth attraction techni☐ues work. That's why so many of the rich and famous continue to use them. But how can you start attracting the wealth you and your family deserve. It's not as hard as you think. These 3 easy techni☐ues are the must-have's of any program to attract wealth.

Wealth Affirmation

To attract wealth, say wealth affirmations every day. In fact, this wealth attraction techni☐ue is super-easy to incorporate into your daily routine. For example, tape a copy to the bathroom mirror and read them over and over as you brush your teeth. Post a copy on the fridge door and make a deal with yourself to read at least 5 wealth affirmations each time you open the refrigerator.

Wealth Visualization

A picture can be worth a thousand dollars if you start using wealth visualization techni☐ues. By imprinting images of you as a wealth attraction magnet, you can set your mind up for success. Visualize yourself receiving a fat bonus check or earning an invaluable business opportunity. Some attraction wealth experts suggest printing a fake check from your home computer that is made out to you and written for an obnoxious amount of money. Tape the fake check where you can see it every day. Imagine yourself opening an envelope and seeing the real thing.

Wealth Meditation

When it comes to attracting wealth, few techniques are as powerful as wealth meditations. By sitting □uietly for about 15-20 minutes and focusing your thoughts and energy on images of your wealth, you can prime your mind so it starts thinking-and feeling-like a wealthy person. And according to the law of attraction, when you start to think like a rich person, you'll start to attract money like a rich person.

Wealth meditations can involve focusing on a single wealth image, for example, you cruising in the anti□ue motorcycle you always wanted. You can focus the meditation on repeating a single affirmation, such as "I am a powerful magnet and attract wealth wherever I go." Some wealth attraction experts recommend combining affirmations and visualizations for the most potent wealth meditation session.

Attracting Wealth Support System

It can be tough to go it alone, especially when friends and family roll their eyes at your newfound attraction wealth secrets. You don't have to go it alone, however. Find a group of like-minded people who can support you. Consider joining a local entrepreneur's group or an online community of wealth attraction believers. Books and seminars from experts in the attracting wealth field can also provide invaluable support in the form of practical guidance and positive reinforcement.

Wealth and riches are out there waiting for you, so there's no reason to put off incorporating these easy-to-use and no-cost techniques any longer. With wealth affirmations, wealth visualizations and wealth meditations, you can have that house, that car, that place in the sun. Start today.

Ways to Become Wealthy

If you want to become wealthy you must look at those who have already generated wealth, and decide which strategy is right for you. There are about half a dozen ways in which to become wealthy, each with their own positives and negatives. Since there are many different ideas of what represents wealth, let's just say any techni☐ue that allows us to make at least a million dollars from scratch.

You could inherit the money. If you have a wealthy parent this could be a possibility. However, this is obviously not something that is under your control, but is solely based on circumstances.

You could win the money. This again is entirely out of your hands and is strictly based on the luck of the draw. While it is possible to win the lottery it is highly unlikely. It is also something that wealthy people rarely if ever do to accumulate more wealth.

Another way you could achieve wealth is to work at a typical job for many years, save and invest a large amount of what you make. If you can earn a large enough return on your money and allow it to compound for long enough, your money could grow over time and by the time you retire you could end up wealthy.

You could decide to go into a profession that is known to pay extremely well. These might include, becoming a doctor, lawyer, or similar profession. While these can pay extremely well, you will need to spend the time in college learning the trade. This could take upward of 10 years just to get the education re□uired. However, if you can put in the time and become a professional in one of these highly paid fields you could retire wealthy.

You could move up the ladder at a large corporation. This could provide you with an extremely large paycheck, and other bonuses including partial ownership in the company. This will also take time as moving up the ladder could take years, but is a definite possibility to creating wealth.

The final way to create wealth is to become an entrepreneur. Becoming wealthy as an entrepreneur will be based on your efforts, and time. By taking this road to wealth there is not any fixed amount of time it will take you to gain wealth, but will rather be based on your ability to find great opportunities, and put them into action. This is also not based on luck, or circumstances beyond your control, but rather completely based solely on the time and effort you decide to put into it. To become successful as an entrepreneur you must take control over your finances. You should become frugal, and not allow your money to slip away. Find a great opportunity, or even better multiple opportunities, and work hard at building streams of income. The more your income streams you have the better.

Be sure to always spend less than you make or you will never achieve wealth. Take the money that you accumulate and be smart with it. Put away 10 percent of what you earn into savings and never touch it. Invest part of your income. Search out good, safe investment opportunities, and put your money into them. Be sure to diversify your investments. Don't be too quick to jump into the next big thing.

The only option to becoming wealthy that you can completely control is by becoming an entrepreneur. So, if you would like to attain true wealth be sure to:

- Live within your means

- Spend your time, energy, and money in ways that will build your wealth

- Seek out opportunities that work for you

- Save, invest and otherwise keep what you make

11 Ways to Become Rich

1) **Becoming rich by marring someone rich-** This is in fact a famous way to become rich. Many people marry people who are already rich and inherit a lot of wealth. Marrying someone for the wealth may not be the most noble way and may say a lot about a person, yet we hear many cases of this happening in society today.

2) **Becoming rich by being greedy-** These are the rich people everyone hates. They are rich but they don't contribute to anyone's happiness. When someone is greedy invariably they take to the incorrect ways of making money. Deceiving people and breaking laws become a habit. One may become rich by being greedy but it comes at a cost. These people don't have many friends or much peace in their lives

3) **Becoming rich by being a crook-** This is an extension of people who are greedy to be rich. The advanced stage of a person being greedy is becoming a crook. Stealing, corruption, selling illegal substances all can get one rich but is it really worth the risk? Most of the people who become rich being a crook end up in jail or are on most wanted lists.

4) **Becoming rich by being cheap-** This is the most popular attempt to become rich. This is done by living below your means. This path is full of sacrifices and living with no satisfaction. The problem with this path is even though one becomes rich he still lives like a poor man. Saving pennies, hoarding money etc. Many people think this is the best way to become rich, yet in the end they still live poor.

5) **Becoming rich by working hard-** Yes, we all believe in this path don't we. In fact we are all taught this from childhood by parents and teachers all alike. This path is followed by most of the middle class people who want to be rich. The path invariably makes you find a job and keep working very hard to earn money. The problem with this is that hard working people often find it hard to enjoy the hard earned money. This is because most of the time is spent working hard for money. Also the people who work really hard at jobs are taxed the highest.

6) **Becoming rich by being exceptionally gifted-** Tiger woods, David Beckham, Cristiano Ronaldo, Lionel Messi, Brad Pitt just incredibly talented, handsome or gifted people who exchange their talents or looks for money. Hollywood, athletes fall in this space. Yet it is also interesting how many people after their careers go broke. Yet if you have are gifted and you know how to make use of your talents or know to market your looks, you can become rich.

7) **Becoming rich by being lucky-** Again this is a popular attempted way to get rich. People spending money on betting, race tracks, lotteries, casinos etc. People here trust their gods and stars than their talents. More often these attempts fail. Only a few are successful in becoming rich following this way. Studies also show that this way of getting rich becomes an addiction and people end up losing money and health.

8) **Becoming rich by inheriting money-** Inheriting property and wealth is also one of the ways to getting rich. Unfortunately in today s world, people kill for inheritance. A rich mans son will inherit all the property after his father passes away.

9) **Becoming rich by Investing-** A very productive way to become rich is by investing. Most cases re☐uire you to have money to invest. The biggest hindrance following this way is also the lack of financial education and intelligence. One can invest in businesses, stocks and real estate to get rich.

Yet if one does not know how to invest properly and manage his finances there is a good chance of incurring losses than profits. If one has the required knowledge you can become rich very soon and by using valid means.

10) **Becoming rich by building a business-** This is the proven and trusted way of becoming rich. Most of the rich people in the world are people who own and have built businesses. This is also one of the best ways to become rich as businesses focus on building systems which mean that the systems operate to make you rich. When a business is built you now own an asset which keeps making money for you. A small business can be differentiated from a large business by the size of the network. Ex: McDonalds is a big business. Simply put people have become rich by learning to build businesses.

11) **Becoming rich by building a Network marketing business-** This is a new age way of becoming rich and its revolutionary. The major difference between the top ten ways and the network marketing business is that the network marketing business focuses on a lot of people becoming rich instead of just one. In today's world, the network marketing business is one of the fastest way to share wealth. The network marketing system does not care of your education, sex, religion, skill set etc. Anyone who has the drive and determination is bound to succeed in this business. The initial joining fees is also low, making it perfect for anyone to make the transition to being an entrepreneur. The icing on the cake with this business, one becomes rich by sharing, teaching and helping others get rich.

Learn How to Explode Your Wealth Fast

Keeping an open mind to new wealth building trading ideas is just as important as finding a new developing trend if you happen to miss that trend prior to it happening. To explode your wealth into serious money, most of the time you need to spot the major trend reversal before it happens, but that is not always the case. Long trends do exist. The key is to know what to do and when if and where you find them and it really does not matter if that trend is going up or down.

Long trends in different commodities can make you rich. Just look at gold and crude oil for example. Even if you caught either of these trends late, you still had a better than average easy chance for a high degree of wealth if you know what to do, where to do it and how. You and you along are reasonable for wealth in your life and it is up to you to get a positive mind set and the correct education to make it happen. The link at the end of this article can lead you to discover the right trading educational plan for wealth building in your life.

Actually, you do have a good chance for true success if you simply apply certain skills by learning new and improved trading knowledge from the pending stock market crash due mainly to the credit and real estate mess of today. With that said, you need to learn about the US Financial Crisis of 2007. The fact is, all you need is the correct knowledge to create serious wealth.

How To Get Rich In A Short Period Of Time- Building Wealth

How to get rich in a short period of time is what most people are looking for these days. However, most people today have an anti☐ue view of personal finance. Simply put, they are passing on to their children the financial advice that their parents once passed on to them. But most of these people are not in a better financial position than their parents were. Why repeat the mistakes of the past? If it did not work then, it certainly will not work now. The crystal ball shows that the financial world is changing at an accelerated speed before our very eyes.

If being wealthy is a desirable position to be in, then it's safe to say that one cannot garner wealth solely on a nine to five job. There needs to be some kind of passive income in place, that re□uires little or no effort from you. That passive income could be an online business or investment such as a guaranteed investment certificate. These are types of passive income that can generate income for you while you sleep.

Debt is a disease and if you are not careful it will slowly eat away at you, leaving nothing recognizable. Debt has brought many people to their financial graves. If you're in debt, then you're in bondage. This is a state of emergency, that requires immediate attention. If your desire is to be wealthy, and you're currently in financial distress, the first thing you need to do is understand your cash flow. Many people fall deep into debt because they don't have a handle on their cash flow.

You would be surprised how small steps could lead to big savings. For example, you are headed to the mall, you leave your credit and debit card at home, and you keep a monthly allowance at home to avoid going back and forth to the bank.

When it is finished, discipline yourself to wait until your next allowance. These are small steps, but they can add up to large savings.

If you want to know how to get rich in a short period of time, you need to know that it will take discipline and commitment to the cause, passive income and savings. If these four cards are brought to the table, the sky is the limit. You're as strong as your weakest link. If your commitment is weak, you will not make it. If you are not willing to discipline yourself, then a lack of discipline will be your downfall. It all boils down to, how much do you want to become rich. If you think the task is too great for you, then you are already defeated. You'll be surprised at what you can do once you put your mind into it. The mind is the most powerful tool of the human body. Train it right, and become the captain of your destiny.

Finding Ways to Become Wealthy 3 Ways to Start With

Wealth is one aspect of life that most people would want to achieve success with. Sometimes being wealthy is taken as an ultimate goal for many and in fact, many also equate much wealth with happiness, thus many people are on the hunt for the ways to become wealthy and rich.

Although it does not necessarily mean that happiness comes from being wealthy in life, it helps a lot to be free from financial woes and worries from time to time. In these times where more and more technology has been developed, it has also given us more things to pay with money that in fact, living with the very basics can still mean spending a good amount of money as well.

If you have been wondering what can make you wealthy and rich, here are some simple ways to become wealthy and rich. They may not make you into instant millionaires, but they can be pretty good start on how to be free from financial worries all the time.

1. **Start your own business.** Most wealthy people have their own business and you can also follow these proven path towards being wealthy. However, putting up a business may not be a surefire way towards being wealthy. There are risks and uncertainties along the way that you have to tackle and face.

If you want this road to be financially wealthy, then you have to prepare yourself for the challenges of managing your own business wisely. Not all businesses succeed, thus be sure that you start right so you will also pave the way which will lead you to financial success.

2. **Get into trading.** Whether it be trading stocks or trading currencies, becoming a trader is said to be a good venture to make good profits. However, as the stock market and the currency market can be very volatile, it is also important to keep in mind that these ventures can also be very risky. In fact, these ventures are not for everyone. You have to have what it takes to become a good trader to be able to succeed in this profitable but highly risky business. Indeed, these can be good ways to become wealthy but always assess yourself first if you have the right attitude, the right investments and the right skills to be able to trade wisely, gain profits and not lose everything you have instead.

3. **Get into real estate.** The real estate business is said to be a good venture if you want to make good money. Of course, the property market provides a lot of opportunities for your capital to grow, double, triple and so on. However, developing properties is not without any risk however. The property market also has its own risks and uncertainties but of course, in the long run, you can actually accumulate good wealth in the real property business. Of course, it helps to learn the ins and outs of the trade and you have to also outsmart competition as this can be a highly competitive venture as well.

These are just three of the ways to become wealthy. In fact, there are a lot of ways to be able to accumulate wealth the legitimate way of course. Do your research and learn from those who have good lessons to share in wealth building.

Easy Ways to Create Wealth From Your Home

Many world economies are in decline, and the outlook for jobs are not good either. As a result of this, many individuals are looking for ways to create wealth. There are plenty of methods to create wealth, whether part-time or full-time, on-line or off-line. For example, you may start by saving some money from your monthly salary, then investing the same in legal investment programs.

Wealthy people find it easier to multiply their earnings. The same is not true however, when it comes to ordinary working-class people. Since they are not wealthy, they do not necessarily have exposure to the better opportunities available to high net worth persons. Such people often fall prey to unsafe investment schemes and end up losing their hard-earned money.

The question regarding the most secure ways to increase your net worth still haunts many people, who aspire to make some additional money. Apart from hard work, you will have to invest your money in a wise manner also. There are various ways to increase your personal wealth, and yet avoid the pitfalls that often beset people who are less informed.

Tips to Create Wealth Securely:

Create wealth with the help of bonds and stocks: While investing in various stocks and bonds, it is very important to educate yourself about the terms and conditions of the schemes regarding the concerned bonds or stocks. If you are not comfortable doing this yourself, you can turn to professionals who will help you, for a fee. If you take a chance without educating yourself, you could lose your money.

Real Estate: Real estate is also an excellent method for creating wealth. You need to make yourself aware of the fluctuating trends in the real estate market. Usually, you will find people purchasing foreclosed homes, renovating them, and then reselling them to gain maximum profits. All real estate experts agree on one thing however. You make your profits when you buy, not when you sell.

Rent a property: This is also a secure way to create some wealth. The most important thing you will have to consider here is, the purchase price. Purchasing an investment property when the market is down may sound smart but you have to be sure whether the market has bottomed out, or whether it is still declining. A wise choice is to purchase investment properties when prices are rising.

Affiliate marketing or network marketing: Another way to create income and grow your assets that people often ignore is creating wealth online through affiliate marketing or network marketing. Nowadays, you will find that colleges in various parts of the country have included network marketing as a subject in their courses.

This shows the importance of network marketing as one of the most effective tool for building a sound financial base.

You will become more adept at handling money as you learn about more ways to create wealth. Always ensure that the money making venture, you are operating is completely legitimate and real, and that you actually spend less than you earn.

Wealth   Beyond Reason

Wealth Beyond Reason is a program that Bob Doyle founded in 2002. Bob's Wealth Beyond Reason program has helped thousands of individuals throughout the world begin creating lives of prosperity and abundance.

Bob Doyle is a very respected author and teacher of the metaphysical principles that surround the Law of Attraction. Mr. Doyle is considered to be one of the leading authorities on the Law of Attraction. Today, Bob considers himself to be a facilitator.

Bob's personal journey is the catalyst for his "Wealth Beyond Reason" program. By 2002, Bob hated his job and felt as if he was dying inside. He quit his job in January of 2002 and had no replacement for it.

Bob Doyle spent the next few months trying to force things to happen. Although Bob knew the Law of Attraction principles in his head, he had to let go and begin letting the universe provide directions for him to take. It was then that Bob really began using the Law of Attraction. Everything Bob Doyle learned is rolled up into his "Wealth Beyond Reason" program.

You might recognize Bob Doyle from the hit movie, "The Secret". This movie helped the mainstream open their eyes and catch a glimpse of the Law of Attraction. The Law of Attraction has everything to do with Bob's program, "Wealth Beyond Reason".

It is through the Law of Attraction that we all create the world we live in. Our lives are played out by what we attract into them. "Like attracts like". This is the Law.

Not too long ago, a few Quantum Physicists stumbled into the world of sub atomic particles and discovered the Law of Attraction is very real. This law was known for a few thousand years through metaphysical teachings. All science did was to verify these principles.

Bob Doyle created "Wealth Beyond Reason" so we all might discover and learn for ourselves how to harness the power of the Law of Attraction. The key to this uni☐ue program is using the Law of Attraction in conscious, positive ways so we can begin living life more abundantly.

Most of us live out our lives almost by chance. When things go wrong, when there is not enough money to pay the bills, we feel a lack. "Wealth Beyond Reason" wakes us up.

When we feel needy, this is what we send out to the universe. The Law of Attraction will send back more of the same thing. Bob Doyle's program takes "lack" out of the e□uation for us.

Bob Doyle's program shows us a better way to communicate with the super conscious universe so that we begin to get a more positive return from it. This unique program, "Wealth Beyond Reason", teaches individuals to utilize this scientific principle to change every aspect of their lives for the better!

This amazing program will demystify the Law of Attraction and eliminate blocks that have been in the way of peoples success, allowing these principles to begin working for them.

Wealth Beyond Reason Make You Rich?

Wealth Beyond Reason is a Complete System for Manifesting Wealth

This program is based on the law of attraction which is a universal law that you can learn to apply to create money, other things and also desired experiences in your reality.

The law itself is easy to learn and understand, but it is learning exactly how to use it and apply it purposefully that can be difficult. Bob teaches you how to master this so that it becomes an effortless and almost automatic process in your life.

You will notice the difference in his course almost immediately. It is not just a book. It is not just an audio. It is not just a coaching program and it is not just a community of students and teachers. It is all of the above.

And this comprehensive and ongoing process of wealth education and applying it consistently is what will make you successful in creating wealth beyond your imagination in your life.

Much of what he teaches will shatter your illusions about wealth and happiness. But this breakthrough process will free up your energy to create the real life you want.

He does not just teach theories and he does not go right to methods and processes. He takes a holistic approach by explaining to you what the law of attraction is. Then he teaches how it works and why it works to create wealth and other desired experiences.

Once you understand this, he provides additional resources such as audio seminars, exercises and even meditation tool to help train both your conscious and subconscious mind to work for you.

Conclusion About Wealth Beyond Reason

The reason this program is so good at what it teaches is because the creator behind it, Bob Doyle is so serious and genuine about wanting to truly help you to achieve the life you want.

He has left nothing out and he backs his course not only with coaching tele-seminars and support but a full money back guarantee. Anyone who is truly committed to manifesting a better life will succeed using his course.

The Easy Way to Creating Wealth

CREATING WEALTH

One of the easiest ways to create wealth is through finding a mentor. Who is a mentor?" A mentor is an experienced person who advises and helps somebody with less experience over a period of time". The experienced in this definition is the mentor and the less experienced is the protégé or mentee.

There is nothing new under heaven. There is nothing you and I want to do or become that somebody, somewhere as not done before. All you need do is find that man or woman who has created or who is creating wealth doing what you intend to do and align yourself with them.

Once you have located a mentor in your quest to create wealth, your next assignment is to become a student of how they do their business. Be humble to be able to pick their secret of wealth creation in that particular area of your interest. The truth of the matter is that when you model someone, you invariably get the same result they have.

Thomas Edison said "if i see farther, it's because i stand on the shoulder of those who have gone ahead" this friend is one of the greatest secret of the world greatest men. It's better to learn by examples than to learn by experience.

Learning from mentors comes in different ways. You can learn from your chosen mentor either through reading their books,listening to their tapes or attending their seminars. You don't need a special gift to model anybody just willingness and a open mind. You will be shock how easy it is to accomplish your dream to create wealth when you heed this seemly simple step. Wealth is your birthright, go for it.

Creating Wealth with Making Money Online

Contrary to popular belief building a successful Internet business is not easy, it is not a get rich overnight scheme. If it were that easy to make money online, then everyone would be out there making millions. The truth is, there are prerequisites, things you must learn, before you can be successful, jump right in unprepared and you will be in for a rude awaking. Believe me I have done it in the past, forget what the Gurus preach about overnight success.

Success is certainly achievable.. but not overnight, the whole process can be demanding, most often a lending hand is all that is required to avoid the pitfalls.

It is clearly possible to gain wealth and become filthy rich "□uickly" if one is prepared to accept very high levels of risk investing in business such as franchise or new startups and other schemes. Wealth - could well be described as being successful, living and enjoying a satisfying and comfortable lifestyle, financial freedom, admiration and respect from friends and relatives.

An important factor separating winners from losers is debt. It is so Important to understand the concept of income and expenditure- avoid personal borrowing this is an absolute mistake.

Unless this is a significant move such as acquiring a mortgage to purchase real estate. Other wise make sure that your personal possessions are owned without obligation.

Three unavoidable principles of life that we must abide by - the past, the present, and the future. By reflecting upon the past, this allows us to avoid pitfalls and steer towards our goals more accurately. The future of course allows the opportunity to dream and set our goals, plan our strategy and take action. The present is the key, it is the time that action must be defined and executed and results established. Getting rich □uick is achievable, but only those with a burning desire to be rich will succeed. (don't even try to fake the desire!)

There are thousands of people with successful online businesses making vast amount of money online daily, membership sites can be a great starter point as they offer very easy-to-follow training programs to help you to succeed with Internet marketing.

Creating Wealth - Using the fast lane..

Pause for a moment. Stay with me on this you won't regret it.. Think about some of the super rich and influential people around today, they all have one thing in common, the desire to be wealthy and stay wealthy, most importantly they are members of very elite clubs and societies, with top notch mentors at their disposal Why?, because the benefits are ten fold, - if in doubt do your research you will see clearly the reasons why wealth building members clubs is really a no Brainer.

Money making mentorship clubs

There are money making clubs that provides a safe haven where members can build mutually beneficial long-term relationships to help one another better achieve each their goals, desires and dreams. These clubs allow you to realize your desire to make heaps of money without spending a fortune. Money making clubs is the fast lane to serious money with all the startup headaches eliminated, this gives you a chance to focus on your main objective.. Making Money..

However, It should be understood this is a serious wealth building business, where You will learn the true insider secrets of the filthy rich shared only amongst the club members. these are not a Mickey Mouse operation, it is only by recognizing and treating this as a real business that you will be successful. Remember; -Be Open To New Ideas! keep your mind free of negative things which will bring you down Success and happiness are partners, stay focused realize that not every outstretched hand is genuine,

Do Your Due Diligence..

Member clubs and programs are not for everyone and may not be for you, if you are still motivated, and who wouldn't! Then this article might be helpful in looking at the online business in a different light.

Today is that day.

If you would like to have the opportunity to have some of the most successful people in the world personally help you achieve financial freedom, Imagine having a monthly income of $5k, $10k, or even $20k Per Month, recurring, month after month after month. How would your life be different?. Chose a money making members program wisely, must have a proven track record and a reputation of excellence, the get rich opportunity is real; the results are achievable.

Lastly, don't believe all that the Gurus proclaim - make $50K per month, it ain't gonna happen right away, you have to be a seasoned pro to make that amount. A modest $3-5K per Month as a starter, then WORK on building your empire to eventually get you to that $50K per Month. Today Is Your Day!

The Easiest Way to Become Wealthy Online

You've finally taken the plunge and decided to try your hand at Internet marketing. OK so far, but would you like to know the easiest way to become a millionaire online? Of course you would. Who wouldn't? You won't get rich overnight but it is possible to become successful internet marketer in one year.

And internet marketing is definitely the fastest way to achieve success online. No doubt about it. For a start, you don't need a stack of expensive equipment and gadgets. Just a computer will do. What's far more important than what's on your desk, though, is what's in your mind and in your heart.

What you get out of a web marketing venture depends on what you put into it. A lot of people never give it a go because they don't know about the easiest way to get a great result in online marketing. It's actually a win-win situation, because the easiest way to make massive cash online is also the fastest way to become a millionaire. And it doesn't entail throwing bucket-loads of cash into your venture.

Sure, you will have to put time and effort into it if you want it to succeed, but once you know the easiest way on how to make massive cash online, you can't to wrong. But if you want to make a big impact on your online marketing campaign in one year, you need to adopt the right approach. Follow in the same footsteps as those who already know the fastest way to become a millionaire.

Many newbie online marketers, however, don't take the right approach. And they fail. You don't have to be like one of these people, if you really want to find the easiest way on how to make money online fast. What distracts many people from their objective of learning how to be successful in the first year is the sheer volume of information on the subject, which can baffle and overwhelm the newbie.

The secret to finding the easiest way how to make money online fast is to take a look at how ordinary people have already achieved that goal. Always be prepared to take advice from someone if you know they have already discovered the easiest way to get great results and create wealth in the first year of your online marketing campaign. Along the way, they will have learned from their own mistakes - and so can you.

How to Build Wealth By Knowing Exactly What to Invest On

Knowing how to build wealth is all about knowing what to invest in, when to invest in it and when to move your investments out of that investment and into another. Wealth building experts know this, and that's how they can prosper in spite of what the economic conditions might be.

The problem for most of us is that it's hard to find the real experts (aka, wealthy people) and to get access to the information which they're using to build financial security. This is why many people are left out in the cold, begging for the crumbs which call from the table of the wealthy. If you're tired of begging and ready to take your place at the table, take three minutes to really absorb what you're about to read.

The Secret to Knowing What to Invest in and When to Invest.

Since the beginning of human civilization, the transfer of wealth has followed a predictable pattern. Those who understand the underlying principle which creates this pattern are the ones who end up accumulating large amounts of wealth while the hard working majority stands by in wonder and frustration. The principle I'm talking about is human behavior.

While everyone is a unique individual with their own unique set of values, we are all driven by a few simple fundamentals of human nature. The most important of these is our desire to avoid pain and to pursue pleasure. What does this have to do with knowing what to invest in and when to invest?

It has everything to do with it because human nature determines the standards by which people make decisions about how to spend and invest their money. People who accumulate large amounts of money can examine the conditions of the economy, and based on their knowledge of human behavior, predict where wealth is about to flow. The ability to do this is more valuable than having a crystal ball which gives you the winning lottery numbers.

This is why understanding the principles of human behavior which determine the flow of wealth is the first step to thinking like a wealthy person, and the first step towards wealthy building.

How to Build Wealth When You Have None to Build With.

You can start building wealth right now, even if you have zero dollars in the bank by doing one thing: educating yourself about how to build wealth by understanding the role human behavior plays in governing the flow of wealth. As you are reading this, the largest transfer of wealth in human history is about to take place, but we're also headed for what might be the most pressing financial crisis ever. Some will become incredibility wealthy, and others will be plunged headfirst into poverty.

Which side of the fence you're on will be determined by what knowledge you're working with when the transfer begins. As the saying goes, luck is no more than preparedness meeting opportunity. An opportunity is coming, and those with the specific knowledge of wealth building based on human behavior will come out victorious. If you'd like to be included in this group, I'd like to invite you to take the next step in learning about the timeless principles of wealth building.

How to Use Wealth Cycles to Profit During Tough Economic Time

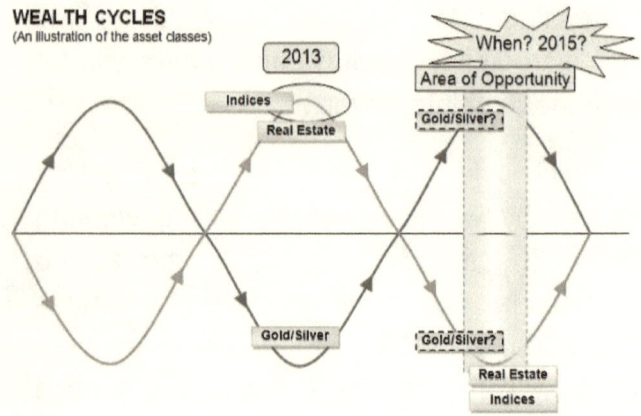

WEALTH CYCLES
(An Illustration of the asset classes)

2013

Indices
Real Estate

When? 2015?
Area of Opportunity
Gold/Silver?

Gold/Silver

Gold/Silver?
Real Estate
Indices

The rules are changing on how we make and invest our money. What worked for our fathers will no longer work in today's society. In fact, what worked only a few years ago will no longer work today. The "information age" has changed just about every aspect of our lives. It has affected the way we shop, the way we communicate, the way we work, and also the way we invest.

With electronic information everything is happening at hyper speed and if you're not monitoring it every second you could lose it all in the blink of an eye. On top of this, we are facing a global economy that is in total disarray with huge debt issues, crooked politicians, and greedy businesses that are all out for themselves. Unfortunately, it is only going to get worse before it gets better. So how can we take back control of our life and right the ship? What can we do to position ourselves to take advantage of the tough economic times ahead? How can we lower our risk and at the same time preserve our capital or even increase our capital allowing us the freedom to make a difference in people's lives?

The answer is Wealth Cycles. What are wealth cycles? Simply put, a wealth cycle shows how you can move your money from an over-valued asset class that's at the peak of its bubble, to an undervalued asset class that's on the way up. Then ride the new asset up until it becomes over-valued, sell, and repeat the process. So the key becomes knowing what asset classes are undervalued and on their way up and put your money WISELY into these areas.

Once again we come back to the "information age" where we need to rely on good ◻uality information to help us make good decisions about our future. By following these cycles we can avoid the violent day-to-day swings of the current financial world and in doing so greatly reduce our risk and preserve our capital. I am all about Protecting and Growing my wealth. In that order, protect then grow.

So, let's look at the 4 asset classes that we need to focus on:

1. **Paper Money** - currency, stocks, bonds, mutual funds, your bank, etc. With all the volatile ups and downs of the market this is not a low risk area that I currently want to be in. I have just recently recovered from my losses from the crash of 2008 and I don't want that again. The days of picking a good stock and going for the ride is gone. There are too many extraneous things that can affect the market that are out of my control. My goal is to take back control not give it up.

The only asset in this class that I am interested in is the Bank of You also known as Infinite Banking. When setup properly this bank can provide you with the funds you need to buy a car, a house, start your own business, or take advantage of great investment opportunities when they arise. This Bank of You also will provide you with a guaranteed tax free retirement income starting at 60 years of age. Yes, tax free. It will also pay your heirs when you die. Now that's a winning trifecta.

2. **Commodities** - Gold, silver, copper, oil, soybeans, sugar, etc. When fiat currencies fail, which they have 100% of the time, precious metals like gold and silver benefit. Despite all-time highs for gold, when you compare it to the Dow or Real Estate it is undervalued. When we look at the current low supply of silver in the world and its historical value in relationship to gold we can see that silver is priced very low. With the current global debt crisis and countries continuing to print more and more money history will repeat itself and the dollar and the market will tumble and the greatest transfer of wealth in history will take place. People will be flocking to gold and silver but it will be too late. It's time to sell.

3. **Real Assets** - Real Estate. The Real Estate bubble busted several years ago and is continuing to decline in a lot of markets. However in some markets, mostly in the Sunbelt areas are doing □uite well. There are some great opportunities in Real Estate right now if you know what to look for and how to structure the deal for a "worst case" scenario.

4. **Business** - Your cash flow generator. Starting a business is the single most important thing anyone can do to improve their financial status and gain control of their destiny. Do it as soon as you can. Starting a home-based business is the ideal route to take in order to keep the startup costs low and the time required to run the business at a minimum. We are moving to the age of self-reliance where we need to be able to generate income on our own and there is no better way than a home-based information publishing business that is centered around what you love to do.

If you are able to focus on positioning your money into the right asset class you will be able to take advantage of the greatest wealth transfer in our history.

What's important to understand, is that this cycle has repeated itself hundreds of times, in hundreds of countries since the dawn of man's first currency.

This time will not be different. It is inevitable, and there's nothing you and I can do to stop it. But with all great change comes great opportunity, and I intend to end up on the winning side.

A great example of this cycle is the Real Estate bubble of the mid 1970's. I remember my dad selling our house in Washington D.C. in September, 1972 and when we returned in June 1973 looking to buy that same house had risen $20,000 in value. Now that may not sound like much but back in 1973 the average annual income was about $12,000 and that house originally sold for $50,000 which makes this a 40% gain in 9 months. I'll take a 40% annual return on my investment anytime. The housing bubble continued until interest rates climbed so high that very few people could even qualify for a loan.

Needless to say, if you had your money in Real Estate you would have done very well. However by the mid 1980's people were walking away from their homes and giving them back to the bank because it was worth less than what they paid for it. Not a good time to be selling this asset class.

Once again Real Estate came back in late 1990's and early 2000's and started to rise rapidly again as we experienced the largest housing boom in history, but then it peaked in 2007 and has been mostly in a downward spiral ever since. Now the money is pouring into the next sector... Precious metals.

If you understand where the current cycle is, you will get rich by selling at the top of the current one, and buying at the bottom of the next.

Unfortunately, the uneducated public does the exact opposite. They buy the assets that are hot and rising, and then sell in a panic at a loss, not realizing that the cycle has ended and that the smart money has already moved on.

However, if you have the right information and the right team assembled it makes it much easier to know when and what to buy and when to sell. The rich and powerful have the best and most talented minds working for them. The wealthy continue to focus on what they do best and what they are passionate about and they let their team of experts do what they do best, grow their wealth.

The smartest thing you can do is to educate yourself so you can make your own decisions about what is best for you. Take control of your financial destiny and assemble your team of financial experts that will work for you to help you grow your wealth. You don't need to know how to do it yourself; you need to know someone that can do it for you.

Instead of you working for your money, make your money work for you.

www.ingramcontent.com/pod-product-compliance
Lightning Source LLC
Chambersburg PA
CBHW021307190526
45164CB00006B/189